This edition published 2005 by
Mercury Books
20 Bloomsbury Street
London WC1B 3JH
ISBN 1-904668-78-X

Publisher: Felicia Law
Design director: Tracy Carrington
Project manager: Karen Foster
Author: Gerry Bailey
Editor: Rosalind Beckman
Designed by: Jacqueline Palmer
assisted by Simon Brewster, Will Webster
Cartoon illustrations: Steve Boulter (Advocate)
Make-and-do: Jan Smith
Model-maker: Tim Draper
Photo studio: Steve Lumb
Photo research: Diana Morris
Scanning: Imagewrite
Digital workflow: Edward MacDermott

Printed by D 2 Print Singapore

Photo Credits
Bettmann/Corbis: 6b.
BSIP/SPL: 34b.
Philippe Gontier/Image Works/Topham: 30bl.
David Grossman/Image Works/Topham: 22bl.
Willie Hill Jr/Image Works/Topham: 25tr.
Image Works/Topham: 14br.
Natural History Museum, London: 41tr.
PA/Topham: 18b.
Photri/Topham: 26bl, 37tr.
Picturepoint/Topham: 5t, 9tr, 21tr, 29tr, 33tr, 38bl.
H Rodgers/Art Directors & Trip: 10b.
Science Museum, London/HIP/Topham: 13tr, 17tr.
Joe Sohm/Image Works/Topham: 42bl.

Crafty
Inventions

HIGH-TECH INVENTIONS

Contents

Mercury Junior

How can I speed up my computer?

In 1642, the French mathematician Blaise Pascal invented the first automatic calculator, using wheels, that could add and subtract. Thirty years later, Wilhelm von Leibniz improved it so that it could also multiply and divide. Could a machine be invented to do more complex calculations?

Advances were made in the mid-19th century, when George Boole combined logic with mathematics, and devised the binary, or two digit, system.

Needing only the '0' and '1' of the system, a mechanical representation could be made very easily. This was the beginning of both computer logic and language.

Meanwhile, in 1801, French weaver Joseph Jacquard invented a loom that used punched cards to make the weaving automatic. His card system inspired Charles Babbage, who developed the 'analytical engine'.

This computer's too slow. There has to be a way to make it work faster.

WHAT HAPPENED NEXT?

- Babbage's 1830s machine contained the basic elements of an automatic computer. Unfortunately, he lacked the funds to develop it.

- Then, in 1891, an American inventor named Herman Hollerith used a punched card system to add up the results of the US census. It worked.

- This led to the first digital computer, built in 1939, followed by the Mark 1 in 1944, which used electromechanical relays, or switching devices. But it was extremely slow.

- A couple of years later, two engineers from the University of Pennsylvania in the US, John Presper Eckert and John Mauchly, found the solution.

Instead of relays, our machine will use 18,000 vacuum tubes. We'll call it an Electronic Numerical Integrator and Computer, or ENIAC. It'll take up 140 square metres of floor space, but it'll be 1000 times faster than Mark I.

ENIAC was the first large mainframe computer. It could do 5000 additions and 1000 multiplications per second.

Solving problems

A **mainframe** computer is the fastest type of computer with the largest storage system. It can solve more complex problems and deal with more information than any other kind of computer. Usually, mainframes are built into a number of large cabinets. The fastest ones are called **supercomputers**.

Very few supercomputers exist because they are so expensive to build. They are found mostly in scientific centres, where they are used by scientists to work on projects such as aircraft design, the development of new drugs or predicting climate change. They can carry out over 12 billion calculations per second.

UNIVAC

ENIAC's big problem was that it took a long time to programme. Eckert and Mauchly had to develop a computer that could store much more of its programming. With the help of John von Neumann, they learned how stored programming would help improve performance. They first built the EDVAC (Electronic Discrete Variable Automatic Computer) machine, which led to the famous UNIVAC I in 1951.

UNIVAC stands for UNIVersal Automatic Computer. Unlike earlier computers, it could handle both numbers and alphabetical characters. It was also the first computer to have separate input and output devices, away from the main computing unit. UNIVAC I was used by many US government departments and huge multinational companies. It was a very popular machine and the last one remained in use until 1970.

ELECTION GENIUS

In 1951, the UNIVAC machine was used to forecast the results of the presidential election in the United States. It surprised everyone when it accurately predicted that Dwight D. Eisenhower would win - just 45 minutes after voting had stopped.

The UNIVAC was the first true mainframe computer.

Inventor's words

ENIAC
EDVAC
mainframe
supercomputer
UNIVAC

Make your own supercomputer

You will need

- selection of small cardboard boxes and tubes, plastic bottles, lids, etc.
- rigid piece of cardboard
- PVA glue
- double-sided sticky tape
- thick card or polyboard
- kebab sticks • scissors
- margarine tub lid
- plastic food tray
- bottle lids • string
- old light bulbs
- old receipts or print-outs
- metallic paints, brush

1 Stick boxes and bottles at the back of a piece of rigid cardboard.

2 For the keyboard, cut square keys from polyboard and 2cm pieces of kebab stick. Glue the sticks onto the square keys.

3 When dry, glue the keys into place onto a large margarine tub lid – the more crazy and ramshackle, the better. Surround the keyboard with a card border for a sunken effect. Glue on to the cardboard base.

4 For the screen, tape a long kebab stick to the back of a plastic tray. Mount a circular piece of cardboard tube onto one of the boxes at the back of the computer and push the stick through the box to fix.

£55.00

5 Complete your crazy computer by adding bottle lid 'switches', coloured string 'wires' and old light bulbs. Decorate with metallic paints. Finally, stick receipts on to the screen for computer calculations!

How can I send a letter instantly?

When Alexander Graham Bell invented the telephone, people could talk to each other over long distances. But if they wanted to write a letter, it had to be sent by post. And that could take days. If only there was a quicker way to send text and pictures.

Alexander Bain, a Scottish physicist, must have felt the same way. In 1843, he made a machine that could transmit text telegraphically. But it didn't work that well.

Other inventors also tried. But getting a letter from one place to another in a flash was a problem. Surely it was possible using electrical signals.

Scientists began to work on the idea that if they could copy the words of a letter and somehow change them into a kind of code, they might solve the problem. Perhaps they should think about using telephone lines...

This letter is really urgent. I want my friend to receive it – NOW!

WHAT DID THEY DO?

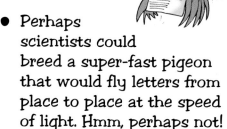

- Perhaps scientists could breed a super-fast pigeon that would fly letters from place to place at the speed of light. Hmm, perhaps not!

- A much better idea might be to use the telephone system. After all, if sound can travel by telephone, why not messages or photographs, too?

- Of course, the words or pictures would need to be changed into electric pulses. But how?

- A copying machine might help. It could scan the paper to pick up tiny differences in light and dark, and turn them into electrical impulses. Perhaps the copier could be combined with a telephone.

Fantastic! The copying machine is changing the letters and pictures into electrical pulses. These will be sent along a telephone line to another machine that will change the electric signals back to the original image. Now, sending messages will take minutes, not days!

In 1966, the first small fax machine took six minutes to transmit a letter. Today's machines can send up to 10 pages a minute.

Exact copies

Fax is actually an abbreviation, or short form, for the word facsimile. It is a message that is sent through the telephone network. A letter or picture is placed in the machine of the sender. After it is sent, an exact copy appears in the machine of the receiver.
A fax machine looks like a small copying machine. But it is connected to a telephone or has one incorporated into it. A user dials a fax number in the same way they would dial a phone number. When a fax arrives, the machine rings like a telephone. And because the fax machine uses the telephone system, the cost of sending a fax is the same as making a phone call.

Light and dark

Inside a fax machine is a special device that is light sensitive. This means it can detect on a piece of paper the amount of light that is coming off it. For example, if the paper has a photograph of a face on it, the light sensitive device will detect all the different light and dark areas on the face as it scans across. It scans many times to cover the whole page.

The amount of light the machine scans is immediately converted into a code. The code is made up of electrical pulses, or signals. The pulses are then sent down a telephone wire in the same way as the electrical pulses that come from sound. At the other end, the fax machine decodes the electrical impulses back into light and dark. Another device prints the light and dark on to a piece of paper. The result is an exact copy of the original.

Sending a message by wire.

WIREPHOTO

From 1935, journalists used fax-type machines to rush important photographs back to head office. This method of sending pictures was called wirephoto or telephoto. The first photograph to be successfully transmitted - an aircrash in the US - took eight minutes to send to 25 cities across the continent.

Inventor's words

electrical pulses
facsimile
fax
light sensitive
wirephoto

Make a fax art frame

You will need

- light and heavy cardboard
- strong glue
- assortment of old or used art materials, e.g. pencils, scissors, paper clips, plastic paint pots, paintbrushes
- plastic pegs • PVA glue
- gold or silver spray paint
- paint and brush
- drawing pins

1 Make a frame by sticking thin strips of cardboard on to a rigid piece of board. Make the inner compartment A4-size so it will hold any fax art you receive.

2 Next fill the 4 surrounding chambers with any old or used art materials you can find, such as felt pens, paint brushes, pairs of scissors. Glue them into place. Dry for 24 hours.

3 Spray-paint the frame gold or silver, or paint with other bright colours.

4 Try faxing a copy of a famous painting to your friends – or even your own compositions. Fix any faxes you receive to your frame with drawing pins.

How can I store lots of data?

When computer chips were invented in 1958 by Jack Kilby in Dallas and Robert Noyce in California, they were developed for use in guided missiles and satellites. Who would have thought that one day, computer chips would be used to operate everyday items from cars to washing machines?

Business is booming. Bosses want to produce more and more, so their employees have to work much harder. But taking on more workers will eat into their profits...

Employers want to make more use of machines. They need the same technological help as the scientists who send rockets into the atmosphere.

How can we use the latest technology to make us more productive – and more profitable?

Best of all, they want a 'brain' that can store information. They could hire robots to do the work. But robots are too slow and cumbersome. Bosses need something that's quick – and which doesn't make mistakes.

WHAT CAME NEXT?

- Engineers had been building bigger and better computers. But there needed to be a new way of thinking. People didn't want huge computers taking up all their space.

- After integrated circuits were invented, computers became much smaller. The circuits contained thousands of electronic parts on a tiny silicon 'chip'.

- Engineers discovered that chips were quick and reliable, and could store lots of information.

- The chip is the brain of a computer. But unlike a human brain, it doesn't make mistakes. It looked as if it could have a great future!

We'll be able to make integrated circuits that are even more powerful and can store huge amounts of data. As a circuit carries out the instructions of a computer program, it will do mathematical and other complex computations.

With the help of microprocessors, modern computers can do a billion different things every second.

Processing data

A **microprocessor** is a type of computer chip, or **integrated circuit**. It carries out the instructions contained in a computer program. Some large computers have more than one microprocessor. Other devices that use microprocessors include digital watches, computer games and microwave ovens.

The microprocessor gets its instructions and data from an external memory device. It performs mathematical and logic operations with the data it is given, and with the data contained in its own memory circuits. When it has finished, it passes the calculated data back to the external device.

Words and bits

Microprocessors have to handle loads of data. The data can't be written in a language such as English and French, though. Instead, it is handled in the form of 'words' made up of a group of 'bits'. A bit is a binary digit, either a '0' or a '1'. Binary simply means counting in twos instead of in tens.

Bits travel through microprocessors in pulses of electric current. So an electric charge in one part of the microprocessor might represent '1', while no charge can represent '0'. The number of bit words a microprocessor can handle determines how quickly it can operate. The first ones used just 4-bit words. Today, they may use 8, 16 or even 64 bits. The pulses of electricity that occur as bits travel through a microprocessor at regular intervals are called clock cycles. Modern microprocessors run at speeds of one million cycles per second, or one megahertz.

A microprocessor runs this computer game.

Inventor's words

binary • bit
clock cycle
computer chip
integrated circuit
megahertz
microprocessor

TINY TECHNICIANS

Since computer chips are tiny, perhaps they should be designed by tiny technicians! In fact, a large master design is prepared on the screen. Then a photographic process reduces the design to a microscopic size. These tiny designs can be used to make hundreds of chips on one wafer of silicone.

Make a microchip maze

You will need

- scissors or craft knife
- cardboard or polyboard
- thick card
- pencil • ruler
- paper • paint
- PVA glue • paintbrush
- marble • acetate
- polystyrene cup

1 Cut out a 16cm-square of cardboard. Next cut some long strips of thick card.

2 Design a simple maze on paper first. Then mark out a small square inside the large card square. Check the pathways are wider than the marble you will be using.

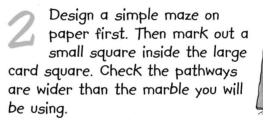

3 Trim the card strips to size, as indicated on your design. Now stick them down, side-on, as shown. Decorate the inside of your maze.

4 Drop a marble into the maze chamber, glue the top of the maze walls and stick on a piece of acetate to seal.

5 Cut off the top of a polystyrene cup and slice through it to make a wrist band. Glue it to the bottom of the maze.

Can computers get any smaller?

UNIVAC I was a huge computer that took up loads of space. It was also expensive. Only businesses and governments could afford to have them. Wouldn't it be great, though, if people could use computers in their own home? But would that mean bigger rooms - or smaller machines?

Computers take up space because they are filled with large pieces of equipment such as vacuum tubes. If only they could be replaced with smaller parts.

Then computers could still do the same job, but not be as bulky. A breakthrough came in 1947, when the transistor was invented.

Just imagine using a computer at home – think how it would change our lives!

The first transistorised computer was made in 1958. But a better system was still to come. A complete circuit was put on to a tiny piece of silicon. By the 1970s, computers could run on a handful of silicon chips.

WHAT HAPPENED NEXT?

- Businesses relied more and more on computers. Companies even linked them together to share information.

- But what was really needed was a small computer for the home that could be operated by people for their personal use.

- Money and cost was always a problem. In 1975, Ed Roberts made a small computer called Altair, but it was only used by computer enthusiasts.

- Two years later a couple of enthusiasts named Steve Jobs and Steve Wozniak decided they could do better...

> We'll build a small, personal computer that's much less expensive than a mainframe, and much easier to use. We'll call it the Apple II and we'll form Apple Computer Inc. to build it. Now anyone and everyone can have their own computer.

The personal computer became one of the most important inventions of the modern world.

Multi-tasking

A **personal computer**, or PC, can be used by one person at a time and will easily fit on to a desktop. Inside, is a tiny **microprocessor**, which contains the electronic circuit that operates the machine. Some PCs have more than one microprocessor: a primary processor, which is a general purpose device; and a **co-processor** that might specialise in mathematics or graphics.

Personal computers use different programs to do different tasks. Most use a word-processing program for communicating. In addition, there are hundreds of specialist programs, including business and finance packages for companies, connection to the Internet – and desktop publishing programs that are used to design books and magazines.

Networking

At home, personal computers are usually operated on their own, But in many offices they are linked together in a network called a client-server network. This is made up of a group of computers connected by telephone, or some other form of communication system, and a powerful central computer.

The central computer is called a server, which acts like a mother ship distributing and gathering information and instructions to and from the PCs it is linked to. These linked PCs are called the clients or workstations. Usually, they are in the same office as the server, but sometimes they may be in a separate building. It is also possible for workers to work from home and send their processed data from there to a server in an office. This type of work is known as telecommuting.

Workers' computers are connected to a server.

COMPUTER ANIMATION

Many of the animated films we see today are made using computer graphics. In a regular animated film, each frame has to be drawn separately. In a computer-animated film, each frame is created separately on a computer screen. In some cases, a frame might require over 5 million calculations.

Inventor's words

client-server
network
co-processor
microprocessor
personal computer
server
telecommuting
workstation

Make your own PC

You will need

- old wiring, microchips
- circuit boards
- plastic tub and lids
- acetate • spray paint
- thick card
- plastic beads
- string • PVA glue
- pipe cleaner
- coloured paper • scissors
- metallic paint, brush

1 Stick some old wiring and a circuit board inside the plastic tub.

2 To make a screen, cut a square piece of acetate to fit over the tub. Spray lightly with paint for a fuzzy look and glue on.

3 Cut a piece of thick card the same size as the tub. Glue on plastic beads and string to make a circuit board. Add microchips and wiring for effect.

4 Make hinges with folded-down card, as shown. Stick them to the circuitboard and screen, then thread a pipe cleaner through them to secure.

5 For the Keyboard, stick a wide piece of card to a plastic lid and make side flaps, as shown. Cut out small squares of paper and stick them on as keys. Add hinges to link to the circuit board and decorate.

Can I make a phone without wires?

With Alexander Graham Bell's telephone came a huge leap in communications. Suddenly, people were able to talk to someone hundreds of kilometres away. Telephones are connected by wires. So it would be impossible to take a phone on holiday or to the shops. Or would it?

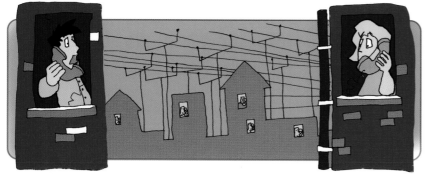

After Bell's invention in 1876, engineers worked to make phones even more efficient. To begin with, each phone user had to have their own outside line.

The overhead wire system was so thick with wires it almost blocked out the Sun! Soon, though, wires were used that could carry lots of signals at once.

If only I could carry a phone around with me all the time. Then I'd never miss a call!

Early phone systems required teams of telephone operators to transfer calls. By the 1950s, the system was automated, and push buttons replaced the dial. But people still had to stay next to the phone to make a call.

WHAT HAPPENED NEXT?

- Bell's phone system directed calls through a system of electric wires and exchange centres.

- Although technology developed over the years, telephones still relied on wires. Some kind of cordless phone would be great. Then it could be carried around the house.

- The development of radio waves to carry sound messages made portable phones possible. But the hand set had to be close to the dial cradle.

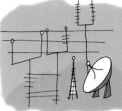

- Then came aerials and satellite technology - and everything changed.

We'll use a large aerial to receive radio waves from a telephone set. But an aerial can only cover a small amount of territory called a cell. So when a user moves out of one cell, the call will automatically be taken over by the next one.

The first mobile phones were used in 1983. They are now more popular than ordinary phones.

Cell phones

A **mobile phone**, or cellular phone, is a telephone that transmits messages using radio signals rather than wires. People can communicate over long distances using a network of antennas and transmitters arranged into small areas called **cells**. The number of cells will vary depending on the size of the network.

Mobile phone callers use a mobile phone unit that is actually a radio transmitter and a receiver. The caller can make and receive phone calls to another mobile phone unit or to a landline telephone unit. The latest generation of mobile phones can make and send pictures, or even short movies.

Networking

Mobile phone callers use a special network in order to make calls. Each network has a central exchange, where calls are collected and transmitted in each of its area's cells.

Most modern mobile phones are digital. This means they send their information in digital, or binary number, code. When a call is made, the message is sent to a transmitter tower – a kind of big aerial. The transmitter passes the message to the network's central exchange. If the call is for another mobile, the exchange sends a message to the other transmitters, which send out a message to find the required phone. Confirmation is then made and the phones are connected. When a phone moves out of range of one transmitter, the exchange connects the call to a transmitter in the closest cell.

PHOTOS BY PHONE

When engineers first talked about phones with a video link, people were nervous about being seen on the other end of a phone. Today, though, we take it for granted. Mobile video phones are a reality. Third generation mobiles allow people to see who they are talking to, as well as to film what is going on around them. And it's all done digitally.

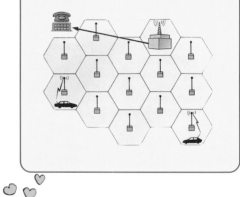

Cell phones have revolutionised the way we communicate with each other.

Inventor's words

binary number
cell
central exchange
digital
mobile phone
network

Make a portable phone booth

You will need

- large plastic cup
- PVA glue
- small cardboard box
- small piece of material
- thin card • scissors
- double-sided sticky tape
- 6 kebab sticks
- clear acetate
- paints, brush

1 Cut the plastic cup into a seat-shape. Glue this to a small cardboard box to create a phone seat. Staple a piece of fabric to the seat and cover with glue to seal.

2 Cut a square of card larger than the seat base. Cut a long strip of card and tape it three quarters of the way around the square piece. Repeat for the roof of the booth, but this time make a border all the way round.

3 Glue a kebab stick into each corner of the base, then glue on the roof. Wrap a strip of card three quarters of the way around the booth, then glue in your phone seat.

4 For the door, attach acetate panes to a stick-and-card structure. Make simple hinges at the top and bottom with strips of card and double-sided tape.

5 Cut the acetate to size and glue window panes all round the booth. Make a card handle and slot it into a cork. Glue on, then paint and decorate your booth.

Can I use lasers to play music?

When Thomas Edison invented the phonograph, people could listen to their favourite music at home. But the sound quality was poor. Also, Edison's recordings were made on cylinders, which were hard to copy from. A better system was needed.

In 1887, Emile Berliner, a German scientist, invented a method of recording on to a flat disc made of shellac – with the help of the Asian lac insect.

Shellac is a plastic-like material found on the shell of the insect. Berliner then invented the gramophone to play the disc on. The sound quality was much better.

Luckily for lac insects, shellac was replaced by vinyl, a plastic material. The sound was 'stored' in a wiggly groove cut into the vinyl, and picked up by a needle on the arm of the gramophone. But was there a better way?

I want to hear music that's clear and pure – just as if I were in a concert hall!

WHAT HAPPENED NEXT?

- A more sensitive needle, or stylus, was used on the gramophone, which produced a better sound. Improved amplifiers and speakers helped as well.

- But there was still some background noise. This was reduced by the invention of the tape cassette. But tapes weren't perfect and tended to wear out.

- Eliminating noise was still a problem, so inventors decided to look at laser technology.

- A laser beam could act like a needle and would neither scrape like a gramophone nor rub like a tape. But how could it pick up sound?

We'll use a digital, or numerical code, represented by a series of dents made in a flat surface. As the laser beam hits the dents, it will change. A sensor will pick up the changes and convert them into electric signals. The signals can then be changed into sound.

A compact disc, or CD, gives much better sound production than vinyl records or tapes.

Easy listening

A **compact disk** is a round, flat platter made of hard plastic coated with aluminium. CDs are usually 12cm in diameter and 1.2mm thick. There is a 15mm hole in the centre. They are generally used to store recorded **stereophonic** music, and are called audio CDs. These can store up to 80 minutes of music.

People can listen to audio CDs in a special CD player or a computer. The first audio CDs were made in Japan in 1982. Another kind of CD, called a **CD-ROM**, can store other information such as files of text, graphics, or pictures, sound and even film. These CDs are usually played in a computer.

Spinning discs

CD sound is carried in a spiral around the disc, rather like the old vinyl records. But instead of grooves, the CD spiral is made up of a series of hollows, called pits. The flat surfaces in between are called flats. The spiral starts at the centre of the CD and runs to the edge.

Pits are just three-fifths of a micrometer across, or about one-hundredth the width of a human hair. There are at least 3 billion pits on a disc, which makes the spiral over 5km long. The spiral, which is on the underside of the disc, is 'read' by a laser beam. As the laser beam travels along the spiral, the light is reflected from the flats and refracted, or spread out, by the pits. Each change is picked up by a sensor, which converts it to an electric signal. The signals are then sent to the speakers, just as with other recording systems.

MINIDISCS

Minidiscs are smaller than CDs. A minidisc recorder will fit into the palm of your hand. It won't hold much computer data, but it will hold 80 minutes of stereo sound. MP3 players are even smaller. They use special 'flash-memory' chips to record music from the Internet. An MP3 player smaller than a pen can hold two hours of stereo sound.

Modern discs can hold hundreds of tunes, and play them back perfectly every time.

Inventor's words

CD-Rom
compact disc
flats
micrometer
mono • pits
sensor
stereophonic

Make a set of CD coasters

You will need

- thick card
- strong glue • cork mat
- bottle tops • scissors
- polystyrene cup
- silver spray paint
- unwanted, damaged or 'freebie' CDs
- 2 small boxes
- paint, brush • thin wire

1 Cut a disk of thick card that is larger than a CD. Glue a cork mat in the centre and 4 bottle tops, as shown.

2 Next, cut thin strips of card into identical pieces and glue them in an upright position to create fins between the bottle tops.

3 Cut the bottom off a polystyrene cup and glue it onto the cork mat. Spray the entire base with silver paint. Now glue a CD on to the cup.

4 Cut the ends off 2 small oblong boxes and make a slit in the sides of each one. Paint and decorate before slotting them onto the CD coaster, as shown.

5 Decorate your hi-tech coaster tray with bits of wire stuck between the fins and the CD.

How can I connect up the world?

Until the 1990s, the telephone was the only way to talk to someone long distance, and faxes were used to send pictures and letters. Both were quick and easy. Modern computers can hold huge amounts of data. Could they be developed to send and receive information even faster?

During the 1960s, the US Army wanted to improve its security systems and develop a communications network that would survive a major enemy attack.

So the Advanced Research Projects Agency, or ARPA, part of the Department of Defence, began working on a network of computers that could 'talk' to each other.

Established in 1969, the system was called the ARPAnet, after the agency. By the end of the year, the computer systems of four universities were able to communicate with each other across the network.

Let's link all the networks across the world together. Then we can communicate with anyone – anywhere.

WHAT HAPPENED NEXT?

- Soon people realised the potential of a vast network. In fact, it would have been difficult to stop its development.

- The idea of a network that stretched across the world, was irresistible, so all the new networks merged with ARPAnet to create a huge supernetwork.

- It was called the Internet, or the interconnected network of networks. But it didn't stop there.

- By the 1990s, anyone who had a computer, modem and Internet software could link up. But Tim Berners-Lee didn't think that was enough...

We need more than text information. I'll write a software program that'll allow sounds, pictures and moving images to be sent on the Internet. I'll call it the World Wide Web. Soon anyone can have a website.

The World Wide Web made using the internet easier and more popular.

Information station

The World Wide Web is part of the computer network known as the Internet. The Web is like a giant encyclopaedia providing text, sound, pictures and moving images. It has multimedia capabilities that can be used for graphics, audio and video. This makes the Internet much more fun. The Web is made up of electronic addresses called websites.

Each site contains Web pages that hold multimedia information. These are stored in computers that are connected to the Internet. An English computer scientist named Tim Berners-Lee, who worked at the European Centre for Nuclear Research in Switzerland, wrote the Web software in 1990. The Web became part of the Internet in 1991.

Web browser

At first, finding information on the Internet could be difficult. It sometimes required complex software or computer commands. The introduction of Web browsers made searching for information much easier. A Web browser is a software package used to find and show information on the Web

A Web browser uses a graphical user interface, a simple way of interacting with the computer using pictures as well as words. The pictures represent commands that are easy to understand. Hyperlinks are also a feature of the Web. They allow users to jump from one document to another, no matter where it is located on the Web. Hyperlinks can carry text, sound or pictures and are created by the author of a Web page.

SUPERHIGHWAY

As the Internet and World Wide Web have grown, they have turned into what is sometimes called the information superhighway. Computers are now linked to telephone systems and television. So people can shop, do their banking, buy a car or even vote on the Internet.

You can do almost anything using the World Wide Web.

Inventor's words

graphical user interface
hyperlink
multimedia
Website
Web browser
World Wide Web

Make a Web showcase

You will need

- empty shoe box
- plastic tub
- oil or acrylic paints
- brush • thin wire
- wire cutters
- scissors
- computer magazines or catalogues
- cardboard

1 Paint the inside of a shoe box black. Paint planet earth on to the inside of a plastic tub, using green, brown, blue, yellow and white paints.

2 Stick your earth to the centre of the box base. With white paint, dot in lots of stars.

3 Make a series of wire circles no larger than the base of the box, then join them with straight pieces of wire to make a web pattern.

4 Insert the web half way down the box. Push the straight wire ends through the sides of the box, then bend and tape down the ends on the outside.

5 Cut out small electronic and computing pictures from catalogues. Stick them on to cardboard backing, then cut out.

6 Tuck all your pictures into the web. Paint and decorate the outside of the showcase.

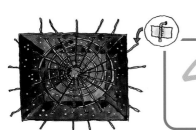

When is a film not a film?

When movies were first invented, some wealthy people had their own cinema rooms in which to watch films. But most people had to wait for a movie to show in their town at the local movie theatre or cinema. Wouldn't it be great if they could watch films at home, too?

In the 1950s, television broadcasters used a special machine to record visual images, using magnetic tape that passed over electro-magnetic posts called heads.

This videotape could record and play back both video pictures and audio sound. It worked even better than photographic film.

Before long, videotape recorders and video cassettes found their way into schools and homes. People could make home movies or watch special programmes. This gave movie people a bright idea...

Why don't we sell copies of our films for people to watch in their own homes?

WHAT HAPPENED NEXT?

- After films had been shown in all the big cinemas, movie distributors decided to put them on videotape and sell them to the public.

- Analogue, or video-disc systems, were also being tested. but people wanted videotape, so cassettes became popular.

- Next, CDs were used for music instead of of tape cassettes. Technology was changing again. But could you put a film onto CDs?

- Engineers got to work. If compact discs could store sound, perhaps it would be possible to store pictures as well.

Look, we can convert images into digital electronic pulses just as we did with sound. So let's make a video disk that works with dents and flats, like an audio CD. We'll be able to store both visual and audio information on it.

Films stored on DVDs have a better picture quality than those stored on tape.

Dents and flats

A DVD, or digital video disc, is a type of CD. It is a thin, flat, round device on which images and sound are stored, or recorded, so it can be replayed on a television set. A DVD is played on a special DVD player that can be attached to a television. Unlike videotape, most DVDs cannot record material; they can only play what has been recorded.

A DVD can hold about seven times more information than a CD. The underside of a DVD is covered in a spiral band of pits, or dents, and flat areas. The pits form a code that is 'read' by a laser beam as it passes over the spiral band. The pits cause a flickering of the beam, which is changed into an electric signal. The signal is then turned into a picture.

33

Digital signals

Manufacturers began working on video-discs in the 1970s. But video-cassette recorders, or VCRs became more popular. It was not until video-discs became digital in the late 1980s that they really began to sell. Recording in digital form made all the difference.

In digital recording, the analogue signal, which means the same as the original signal, enters a recorder through a microphone and camera. The signal can be sound or lightwaves. This signal then passes through a converter that changes the waves into a series of two digits – zeros or ones. The digits are represented by electrical pulses. The pulses are 'recorded' or copied on to a CD as a series of pits or flats, the dents and flat areas of the disc. When the operation is reversed, the disc can be read by a laser and the digital pulses converted back into sound and vision.

An operator creates digital images at a recording studio.

ONE OF A KIND

In the 1980s there were two types of video systems - Beta and VHS, and tapes for one system couldn't be played on the other. Something had to give, and it was the Beta system; everyone uses VHS. DVD makers did not make the same mistake as the video-tape makers, and there is only one DVD system.

Inventor's words

analogue
CD • digital
DVD
flats
pits

Make an acetate picture

You will need

- 3 sheets of acetate
- paint and brush
- cardboard
- hole puncher
- pencil • PVA glue
- wooden chopsticks
- old felt pens
- craft knife • thin wire
- lollipop sticks

1 Paint a picture in 3 layers as follows. Work out a background, a mid-ground and a foreground for your picture, then paint each section on a separate piece of acetate. Leave to dry.

2 Now take a large piece of cardboard to make a backboard and frame for the picture.

3 Put your acetates together and hole punch each corner. Lay them on to your frame and mark an 'x' on the board where the holes are. Glue chopsticks on your 'x' marks.

4 Take apart some old felt pens and cut twelve 2cm spacers from the empty tubes with a craft knife.

5 Push a spacer on to each stick and then alternate acetates and spacers until you have built up your picture. Use wire ties to stabilise the sticks.

6 Paint the base and decorate with painted lollipop sticks.

35

Can I get inside a computer?

Once small personal computers had been developed for the general market, manufacturers soon realised the machine's potential for playing games. The first games were simple, with basic graphics. But they were continually being improved. New worlds were opening up.

Computer games became more and more popular as graphics improved. At one time, Pacman seemed pretty advanced. But soon it was left far behind.

Modern games became more and more exciting. Now games were created with many levels, so each one was a challenge.

It would be much more fun to be 'inside' the computer, than just watching the screen.

But if games could be almost real, would it be possible to create a whole new world inside a computer? Could you actually become part of the game? Some people thought you could.

WHAT HAPPENED NEXT?

- In the 1960s, scientists experimented with ways to interact with a computer program.

- Games-makers produced joysticks and button controls, but that didn't take you inside the game. You still had to watch it on a screen.

- To get into a computer game, a player would need to be digitally reproduced in a smaller size. But surely that was strictly science-fiction?

- Then scientists thought about the senses needed for interaction: eyes, ears and touch. Could these senses be linked up to the computer?

We'll build a head-mounted display that will contain miniature TV screens – one for each eye. This will give a 3-D effect. Then we'll make special gloves, wired to the computer. The result will be virtual reality.

Virtual reality systems were used to create computer-generated worlds in which the player could travel.

Virtually there

A **virtual reality** system is an artificial 3-D environment created by a computer and some other devices. The system uses special **software** to trick the human senses, especially sight and hearing. It tries to create the feeling of being inside the computer, or inside another world. People can look at computer-generated objects as if they were real.

They can also handle objects as if they really existed. Virtual reality systems are not just for fun. For example, they help pilots to learn how to fly without having to go into the air; racing drivers can practise on tracks they have not raced on before; medical students can carry out operations on virtual patients; and the army can recreate a battlefield.

HMDs

Usually, virtual reality systems use a head-mounted display, or HMD. An HMD is a headset or helmet. Inside, are two miniature television-type screens, one just in front of each of the user's eyes. There are also speakers located at the side of the set, one for each ear.

The HMD is connected to the computer. And it is the computer that creates the images. A slightly different image is created for each television screen. When they are seen together, they create a 3-D effect that fools the eye into thinking the image is real. A tracking device, which is built into the HMD, senses the direction in which the user is looking. As the head moves, the computer immediately updates the two images. This gives the impression that the user is looking around inside the computer.

A REAL CAD

Another kind of virtual reality system is called Computer-Aided Design, or CAD. CAD programs enable architects to build buildings on screen, and engineers to build virtual cars. The Boeing 777 aircraft was planned entirely on a CAD system, using graphics and special maths software.

The science-fiction film *Final Fantasy* was the first film to be completely computer generated, in 2001. All the actors were photo-realistic but stiff and expressionless.

Inventor's words

CAD
HMD
software
virtual reality
3-D

Make a VR helmet

You will need

- balloon
- strips of newspaper
- PVA glue • craft knife
- plastic cake tray
- empty sticky tape reels
- cork coaster
- empty yoghurt pots
- bottle lids • thick card
- thick wire • wire cutters
- double-sided tape
- paint, brush

1 Cover a balloon with strips of newspaper soaked in watered-down PVA glue to make a helmet shape. When dry, burst the balloon and trim around the edges of the helmet.

2 Cut a slit in the helmet just above the eyeline and slide in a plastic tray, as shown. Glue it into place so it covers your eyes like a visor. Stick reels onto the front for a goggle-effect.

3 Stick on cork coasters as earpieces, then glue on plastic pots and lids to create large ear units.

4 Cut a slit into some card discs, then cut equal lengths of thick wire and bend as shown. Slide a disc over each foot of the wires.

5 Stick the feet of the wires all around the helmet with double-sided tape. Paint and decorate.

Does a TV need a photon gun?

Ever since John Logie Baird invented the television in 1925, sets have become larger and the quality of the pictures has improved. But television sets are deep, heavy and awkward because of the size of the photon gun. If only there was an alternative device.

The first televisions were small, with little round screens. But viewers were happy to see moving pictures in their own home. Eventually, TVs got bigger.

When black-and-white became colour, the new sets were a revelation. But they were just as heavy and deep at the back as black-and-white TVs.

Digital television gave much better picture quality, and screens started to grow in size. Some looked more like small movie screens. But the same old problem existed. The photon gun took up too much room.

What can I use to make a slim-line version of the television set?

WHAT DID THEY DO?

- Photon guns fire tiny specks of red, blue or green light at a special screen inside the television set. These specks make up the colour picture.

- But a photon gun needs to be big if it's to work properly. So a large part of the television sticks out at the the back just to hold it.

- If only there was another way of getting light on to a screen. Engineers looked at various devices that lit up when electricity was passed through them...

- ...and came up with neon light, which contains gas. What if that idea could be applied to a TV screen?

A gas-filled screen is the solution! If an electric current is passed through the gas, it will give off ultraviolet light. The UV light will then light up fluorescent material on a screen. Result: no photon gun – and a spectacularly thin screen!

Plasma screens are so new they still can have teething troubles. The cells can break easily. So the screen must always be horizontal.

Cells of gas

A **plasma screen** creates pictures using tiny compartments called **cells**. The cells are filled with a gas, usually **neon** or **xenon**, and are positioned between sheets of glass. Long electrodes are also sandwiched between the glass on both sides of the cells. When an electrode causes an electric current to flow in the cell, the gas inside is 'shaken up'.

This gives off energy in the form of ultraviolet light. The ultraviolet light interacts with coloured phosphors in another layer of the sandwich, giving off blue, red or green light. Combinations of these colours make up the colours we see on screen. Plasma screens can be up to 1.5m wide yet only 7 to 12cm thick, and can be hung on a wall.

Fluorescent light

The main element in plasma gas is fluorescent light, or light caused by a substance absorbing radiation. Plasma gas is made up of free-flowing electrically-charged atoms, and electrons, which are negatively-charged particles.

Gas atoms have an equal number of protons, the positive-charged particles in an atom's nucleus, and electrons, which spin around the nucleus. This gives the atom a zero charge. If free electrons are introduced into the gas by running an electric current through it, they bump into the atoms, knocking loose other electrons. This gives the atom a positive charge. All this movement excites the gas atoms in the plasma and they release photons, or bundles of light energy. Xenon and neon atoms give off this energy as ultraviolet light. This can be used to produce coloured light in phosphors, as in a plasma TV screen.

NOT A TELEVISION

Technically, a plasma display is not a television because it doesn't have a tuner. So it can't take signals from an aerial or cable. It's just a monitor. This means it has to be hooked up to a separate unit that has its own TV tuner, such as a VCR.

Inventor's words

cells
neon
electron
photon
plasma gas
plasma screen
proton
xenon

Make a plasma picture

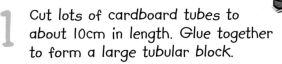

You will need

- selection of different-sized cardboard tubes
- craft knife and scissors
- PVA glue
- PVC tubing or thick stick
- thick card
- poster or picture
- wire
- paint, brush

1 Cut lots of cardboard tubes to about 10cm in length. Glue together to form a large tubular block.

2 Cut a hole at the base of one of the central tubes and attach a rigid piece of PVC tubing or thick stick.

3 Next, cut a large parcel tube in half and cut a hole in the top of it to fit the other end of the tubing or stick. Cover the ends of the half tube with thick card cut to size. Glue the parts together.

4 Cover the front end of the block of tubes with glue and drop the poster or picture on to this -- see that it is blank on the reverse so that the light shines through. When dry, trim around the edges of the tubes with a craft knife.

5 Place your screen in front of a window, or shine a torch from behind, to light up the picture.

Glossary and index

Analogue Analogue means 'similar' or 'alike', and usually refers to the electrical signals that are created directly from other signals, such as sound, rather than from a digital code.

Binary Method of counting made up of binary digits, or 0 and 1. Computers use binary code when making calculations.

Bit Short for binary digit, either 0 or 1.

CAD Short for Computer-Aided Design. CAD programs, for example, enable architects to construct buildings on screen and engineers to design virtual cars.

CD-Rom Part of a computer, CD-Rom stands for read-only memory. The memory circuits contain instructions that the computer needs to work properly.

Cell Part of a network of antennas and transmitters arranged into small areas in a cell phone system.

Cellular phone Mobile phone, or one that uses a system of cells to transmit and receive messages.

Central exchange Each cell phone network has a central exchange in each of its area cells where calls are collected and transmitted.

Client Part of a client-server computer network. This is made up of a group of computers connected by telephone, or some other form of communication system, and a powerful central computer.

Clock cycle Bits travel through a microprocessor in pulses of electricity that occur at regular intervals called clock cycles.

Compact disc Round, flat platter made of hard plastic coated with metal, used for recording music.

Computer chip Integrated circuit that carries out the instructions contained in a computer program.

Co-processor Secondary processor in a computer that might specialise in mathematics or graphics.

Digital Anything that uses numbers, or digits. Data in a computer flows in a code made up of the digits 0 and 1. Digital machines have their input information changed into digital code before the machine uses it.

DVD Short for Digital Video Disk. It is compact disc on which images and sound have been stored, or recorded, so they can be replayed on a television set.

EDVAC One of the first mainframe computers, EDVAC stands for Electronic Discrete Variable Automatic Computer.

Electrical pulses Short charges of electricity sent along an electric wire or circuit.

Electron Tiny speck of matter that is usually part of an atom. An electron moves in orbit around the nucleus of an atom. p.42

ENIAC The first large mainframe computer, ENIAC stands for Electronic Numerical Integrator and Computer. p.6

Facsimile An exact copy. The word was shortened to 'fax' when referring to written messages sent through a telephone network by a facsimile machine. p.9

Fax Written message sent by a fax machine through a telephone system. p.9

Flats Smooth surface of a CD or DVD. p.26, 34

Graphical user interface Method of interacting with the computer using pictures as well as words. p.30

HMD Headset or helmet, also known as Head-Mounted Display. Inside are two miniature television-type screens, one just in front of each of the user's eyes. There are also speakers located at the side of the set, one for each ear. p.38

Hyperlink Means of moving from one document to another no matter where they are located on the Web. p.30

Integrated circuit Also called a microchip, it is a tiny electric circuit that can be fitted into small devices such as computers or calculators. p.13

Light sensitive Device that can detect on a piece of paper the amount of light that is coming off it. p.10

Mainframe Large computer that takes up more space than a personal computer. The largest, most powerful computers can take up a whole room. p.5

Megahertz A megahertz equals one million cycles per second, the speed that bits travel through a modern microprocessor. p.14

Micrometer Instrument used for measuring small lengths or angles. p.26

Microprocessor One or more microchips working together. p.13, 17

Mobile phone Another name for a cell phone. p.21

Multimedia Using more than one kind of media, such as books and videos, to supply information. p.29

Neon Chemical element. It is a colourless gas that glows when electricity is passed through it. p.41

Network Link-up of a number of computers or other devices. p.22

Personal computer Computer that can be used by one person at a time. Even the largest personal computers, or PCs, can fit on to a desktop. p.17

Pits Series of tiny hollows that make up a spiral on a CD or DVD. The pits are 'read' by a laser. p.26, 33

Plasma gas Plasma gas is made up of free-flowing ions, or electrically-charged atoms, and electrons, which are negatively-charged particles. The plasma glows when electricity is passed through it. p.41

Plasma screen TV screen made up of cells containing plasma gas. The gas reacts to electricity causing bursts of light. p.41

Proton Tiny particle of matter that is found in the nucleus of an atom. A proton has a positive electric charge. p.42

Sensor Device in a CD or DVD that recognises light changes as the laser passes over the pits and flats of the disk. It converts the changes to digital electric signals. p.26

Server Central computer in a network of computers. It distributes information and instructions to the other PCs as well as gathering them in. p.18

Software The name given to programs, routines and procedures used to operate computer hardware. p.37

Stereophonic Sound from a sterophonic record or tape comes from different loudspeakers p.25

Supercomputer Large mainframe computer. p.5

Telecommuting The ability to work out of an office due to availability of personal computers. p.18

Telephone Device for communicating over a distance or out of the hearing range of another person. It has a mouthpiece for turning sound waves into electronic signals, and an earpiece that turns the signals back into sound. p.9, 21

UNIVAC Short for UNIVersal Automatic Computer. Unlike earlier computers, it could handle both numbers and alphabetical characters. It was also the first computer that had separate input and output devices. p.6

Virtual reality An artificial, three-dimensional environment created by a computer and other devices. p.37

Web browser Software package used to find and show information on the Web. p.30

Website Electronic address on the Web. Each website contains Web pages that hold multimedia information. Websites are stored in computers that are connected to the Internet. p.29

Workstation Outer personal computers served by the server. In most cases they are in the same office as the server. p.18

World Wide Web Part of the computer network known as the Internet. The Web, as it is known for short, provides sound, pictures and moving images as well as text. p.29

Xenon Element that is chemically inactive. It is a colourless gas that glows when an electric current is passed through it. p.41

Tools and Materials

Almost all of the materials in this book can be found around the house or bought at your local art or craft shop. If you cannot find the exact item, try and replace it with something similar.

Most of the models will stick fast with PVA glue or even wallpaper paste. However, some materials need a stronger glue, so take care when using these as they may damage your clothes and even your skin. Ask an adult to help you.

Always cover furniture with newspaper or a large cloth, and protect your clothes by wearing a work apron.

User Care

Take special care when handling sharp tools such as scissors, pointed gadgets, pieces of wire or craft knives. Ask an adult to help you when you need to use them.